101 Soul Seeds

for Peacemakers & Justice-Seekers

Copyright © Bruce Epperly, 2021.

Bible quotations are from the New Revised Standard Version Bible, copyright 1989, Division of Christian Education of the National Council of the Churches of Christ in the United States of America. Used by permission. All rights reserved. The author has made modest revisions to masculine references in order to be more inclusive in spirit.

ANAMCHARA BOOKS
Vestal, New York 13850
www.AnamcharaBooks.com

Paperback ISBN: 978-1-62524-823-7
Ebook ISBN: 978-1-62524-824-4

Cover design and interior layout by Micaela Grace.
Plant drawings by Microvone (Dreamstime.com).

101 Soul Seeds

for Peacemakers & Justice-Seekers

BRUCE G. EPPERLY

Introduction

As a college student, I recall seeing a bumper sticker that announced, "If you love Jesus, seek justice. Any fool can honk!" Though fifty years have passed since that sighting, I believe that this is still sage advice. Justice is essential to spiritual and ethical maturity. Hearing the cries of the poor and the lamentations of the dispossessed deepens our experience of God's presence in our lives. We can't know God if we turn our backs on the oppressed and forgotten. As the Hebrew prophet Amos warned, apathy and disregard for the suffering of those who experience systemic injustice and poverty lead to a famine of hearing God's word.

It has been said that the difference between ignorance and apathy is "I don't know" and "I don't care." Today, with the 24/7 news cycle, news feeds on social media and phone apps, and print media, few of us can claim ignorance of systemic injustice, environmental destruction, racism, hate crimes toward the LGBTQ community, and inhumanity toward immigrants and political refugees. The question is, "Do we care?"

I believe that healthy spirituality widens our circle of empathy and concern. It deepens our sense of peace despite the chaos of life. God inspires us to prophetic healing that challenges injustice, protests poverty, and confronts apathy, especially among the powerful and privileged, even as we affirm God's presence in oppressor and oppressed alike. Like Jesus, we can grow in wisdom and stature.

Jesus' heart expanded to embrace the whole planet in its wondrous and tragic beauty. He wept over Jerusalem and felt the pain of those who experienced social and religious stigma due to disease, ethnicity, and economic status. Like the Buddhist bodhisattva, Jesus chose to suffer to bring healing and wholeness to wayward humankind. In the words of philosopher Alfred North Whitehead, Jesus shows that "God is the fellow sufferer who understands." Invoking the prophet Isaiah, Jesus proclaimed his mission statement:

> The Spirit of the Lord is upon me,
> because God has anointed me
> to bring good news to the poor.
> He has sent me to proclaim
> release to the captives
> and recovery of sight to the blind,
> to let the oppressed go free,
> to proclaim the year of the Divine favor.
> (Luke 4:18–19)

When Jesus stated that his coming was to ensure that persons "may have life and have it abundantly" (John 10:10), he was pointing toward God's realm of Shalom in which the streets are filled with laughter, food abounds, and love characterizes our relationships. Abundant life must be the reality for all God's children if we are to be fully in sync with God's Shalom.

Today's peacemakers and justice-seekers follow in the footsteps of Jesus and the prophets of Israel and Judah. They embrace the right livelihood and right speech of Gautama Buddha and the creation spirituality of the First Americans. Our quest for peace and justice also emerges from our experience of God's moral and spiritual arcs, embedded in the historical process, and our recognition of the disparity between economics and public policy and God's vision of Shalom.

Prophets are restless. They see an alternative to the injustice and violence of the social order. The discontent and disappointment of those who challenge unjust social structures are often overwhelming apart from firm spiritual grounding. Spiritual practices, resulting in experiences of God's deep peace, lighten our spirits, widen our perspectives, and energize our actions. Experiences of calm emerging from times of prayer and meditation enable us to transcend binary approaches that divide the world into friend and foe and provide strength for the long haul. When we take time to "be still and know that God is" (Psalm 46:10), we tap into the reservoirs of Divine replenishment and resilience to confront the evils of our time. Martin Luther King Jr. took time apart to rent a hotel room for retreats. Mahatma Gandhi joined meditation with activism. Dorothy Day went regularly to Mass and immersed her politics in prayer. We can learn from their example.

Authentic spirituality embeds us in the pain of the world and inspires commitment to social justice and conflict resolution. Rooted in the intricate and dynamic fabric of relatedness of life, authentic spirituality seeks peace and justice in the public sphere, while nurturing a sense of equanimity, self-transcendence, and connection with all creation. Rooted in the deep mystery of God's love, we can face challenge and struggle with confidence that God's vision of justice and peace will outlast the demagogues, dictators, and destroyers.

This book is intended to support your integration of peacemaking, justice-seeking, and spiritual growth. You have a calling to be God's companion in healing the world one relationship, phone call, and protest at a time. The journey may be long and difficult, and the moral and spiritual arcs may be hidden from your view. Patience and resilience are essential for social change agents. But the path of contemplative activism will restore your spirit and give you strength for the journey toward the Promised Land of Shalom.

These 101 "seeds" are undergirded by prayer and meditation. I invite you to integrate the following practices with the reflections in this book: First, breathe your prayers. On Easter night, Jesus breathed on his followers and said, "Receive the Holy Spirit." Take time to close your eyes, relax, and breathe deeply God's Spirit in preparation for each reading. Breathe deeply as you conclude each reading. Second, if you are physically able, take the daily reflections out for a walk. Moving our bodies inspires spiritual movement. As you take a meditative walk, reflect on the insights inspired in your reading, connecting them with your daily life.

You are embarking on a holy adventure with many unexpected surprises, blessings, and challenges. Let us begin our journey with a Celtic blessing:

> Deep peace of the running wave to you.
> Deep peace of the flowing air to you.
> Deep peace of the quiet earth to you.
> Deep peace of the shining stars to you.
> Deep peace of the Son of Peace to you.

— Bruce Epperly
November 24, 2020, the celebration of my sixty-eighth birthday

1.

Jesus said to them again, "Peace be with you. As the Divine Parent has sent me, so I send you." When he had said this, he breathed on them and said, "Receive the Holy Spirit."

—JOHN 20:21-22

Peace is the gift of God's love for us. Peacemaking is God's calling for each of us as well. God sends us into the world to be healing companions and instruments of peace in our families, communities, nation, and the planet. God gives us the resources to embody the arc of Shalom in our world. God breathes on us, in us, and through us,

giving us wisdom, insight, courage, and calm sufficient to respond to life's challenges. The Spirit of God, moving through every life, can energize, comfort, and guide us with every breath. Peace begins with an inner sense of wholeness and calm, and then as we exhale, we recognize that our breath is joined with all creation. We can choose to be God's healing companions, limited and fallible, and yet necessary for healing the soul, the nation, and the planet.

Breath of the Universe, breathe on me, in me, and through me. Calm my spirit and energize my imagination. Let every breath be a prayer and let me be Your companion in the quest for peace and the embodiment of Your Beloved Community in our world.

2.

Breathing in, I feel calm.
Breathing out I smile.

—THICH NHAT HANH

Vietnamese Buddhist monk and social activist Thich Nhat Hanh reminds us that peace is as near as your next breath. Peace begins in the human spirit, mindful of each moment's blessings, aware that now is the moment of healing and salvation. Every breath can be a prayer. Just a few deep breaths can begin restoring us to wholeness in body, mind, and spirit.

Pause a moment right now and breathe deeply. Feel the life-energy of the universe flowing in and through you. Experience the wisdom of God rising up within your thoughts and feelings. Sense your connection with life in its wondrous and tragic beauty. Let your exhaling be a gift to the universe. Out of inner peace, let your smile be the gift of peace to everyone you meet. Let your peaceful spirit calm the waves of anxiety and antagonism of those around you. Joining inner and outer peace, let there be peace on Earth, and let it begin in this holy moment.

Wondrous Creator, thank You for each breath and moment's experience. Let my breathing be a blessing and my actions bring healing to this good Earth.

3.

> There is no way to peace,
> peace is the way.
>
> —A.J. MUSTE

Authentic peace joins our inner life and our outer behavior. The pathway to peace involves self-awareness and a commitment to bringing peace to every life situation. Peace emerges from a calm spirit that recognizes our unity with all creation, beginning with our closest relationships. We recognize that we often fail in our quest to join inner and outer peace. But each moment gives us the opportunity to choose peace again. To love our

neighbor, to recognize the holiness in a political opponent, and to see God's presence in a stranger or foreigner. Peacemakers are not passive. They may challenge, protest, and confront those who promote violence, alienation, and chaos. Still, the path they take is one of love and reconciliation, not the scorched-earth politics of those for whom power and victory are the only values. Our commitment to peace one moment at a time saves our souls and brings healing to the world.

God of Peace and Wholeness, may my quest for inner peace be reflected in my thoughts, words, and deeds. Let Your deep peace flow through me to refresh and renew a troubled world.

4.

Peace is every step.

—THICH NHAT HANH

As he marched with Martin Luther King Jr., theologian and social activist Abraham Joshua Heschel noted that "I felt like my legs were praying." On the walk of life, our commitment to peace can be found in our approach to every situation. Our healing occurs one step at a time.

I am an avid walker. Most mornings, you will find me at a local Cape Cod beach, walking, praying, or simply taking in the beauty of the day. Breathing deeply and mindfully, I discover

that, despite the machinations of political leaders, I can experience God's deep peace. Every step can be a blessing. Every mile can be a pilgrimage of spirit. Every encounter a "thin place," where Heaven and Earth meet. Peace is every step.

With every step, let me grow closer to You, Giver of Peace. Let my heart beat with love. Let my footsteps be prayers. Let my words be healing balm.

5.

Lord, make me an instrument of your peace.
Where there is hatred let me bring love.

—"PRAYER OF ST. FRANCIS"

Our lives are not our own. They are our gifts to God. Each moment's birth emerges from the universe—the impact of our personal history and environment, the swiftly moving planet, the rotations of the solar system, and the energy of the galaxy. All flowing in and through us. Each moment arises from God's intentionality. God's aim toward wholeness and beauty is embodied in every life.

God has a vision for your life. When you pray to be an instrument of peace, you open yourself to God's wisdom and creativity. With openness to God and a desire to embody God's vision, you let go of your ego and discover your unique calling in every situation. You become an agent of God's moral and spiritual arc, practicing peace and bringing healing and reconciliation to the world.

Spirit, make me an instrument of Your peace. That will be enough for me. Let me embody the graces and gifts that transform hatred into love.

6.

What does the Lord require of you
but to do justice, and to love kindness,
and to walk humbly with your God?

—MICAH 6:8

The quest for justice is at the heart of the human adventure. We find wholeness when we go beyond self-interest to embrace the well-being of others. Justice challenges us to promote equality of opportunity for everyone. Justice invites us to uplift the vulnerable and welcome the outcast as God's beloved. Kindness takes us beyond enmity to empathy. To seek reconciliation among foes. To honor the feelings of our companions, whether

teammate or competitor. To provide comfort and support for persons in need. Humility reminds us that we are all connected as children of the Earth. We reach out to one another, embracing our common ground rather than accentuating our differences. We have unique gifts and experiences, worthy of treasuring—but our gifts flourish best when they become gifts to those around us, uplifting and empowering, and joining us in joy and sorrow.

Awaken us, Spirit of Peace, to our common humanity. Awaken us to our common hopes and dreams—and out of that awakening, grant us Your peace.

7.

The wolf shall live with the lamb,
the leopard shall lie down with the kid,
the calf and the lion and the fatling together,
and a little child shall lead them.

—ISAIAH 11:6

According to the Hebraic prophet Isaiah, history is guided, inspired, and judged by God's vision of Shalom. There is a moral and spiritual arc in history that asks us to embody the values of God's far horizon of wholeness. There is prophetic peace, grounded in God's Spirit moving through our spirits. When we pause awhile, even in turbulent times, we will discover a deep peace that passes understanding.

Divine empathy challenges us to break down every barrier that prevents people from experiencing God's abundant life. Whatever stunts a child's imagination stands under God's judgment. The celestial surgeon may cause pain but the pain that comes from Divine challenge promotes health and wholeness. The soul of the nation and our own souls is at stake when we perpetrate injustice. The prophetic remedy, painful as it may seem, brings about a world where enemies become friends, children play safely in the streets, and communities blossom in love.

Adventurous Spirit, inspire my imagination to visualize a realm of justice. May I be Your hands and feet in creating Your realm on Earth as it is in Heaven.

8.

Visualize a golden light within you and spread it out. First to those about you— your circle of friends and relatives— and then gradually to the world.

—PEACE PILGRIM

Mildred Lisette Norman, known as Peace Pilgrim, walked over 25,000 miles from 1952 to 1981 in quest of world peace, crossing every state of the Union with only a many-pocketed apron to carry her scant possessions. She left a promising career in business to share the good news of an alternative reality, in which nations beat their swords into plowshares and transform nuclear weapons into peaceful, safe energy. Peace Pilgrim saw peace as the joining of inner and outer whole-

ness, reflected in peaceful relationships and just social structures. She believed that something of God was hidden in every person. With every breath, the light within joins us with all creation. The light of God is just awaiting our discovery.

Peace Pilgrim's meditation begins with taking a deep centering breath, then visualizing God's light filling you from head to toe, energizing your spirit. As you exhale, visualize God's light spiraling outward to embrace family members, friends, national leaders, and the whole Earth. Conclude by focusing on God's light flowing through you and all creation, affirming your oneness with all creation and your vocation as a light-bearer for God's realm of Shalom. Throughout the day, look for the light in yourself and everyone you meet.

Parent of Light and Love, let Your light shine in me.

9.

[Abraham Joshua Heschel] was once asked why he was demonstrating against the war in Vietnam. He replied, "I am here because I cannot pray." When his inquisitor asked, "What do you mean . . . ?" Heschel replied, "Whenever I open the prayer book, I see images of children burning from napalm."

—SUSANNAH HESCHEL

Prayer is not an escape from life's problems. Prayer embeds us in the pain of the world. It sensitizes us toward the experiences of forgotten and oppressed persons, who have their backs against the wall. Prayer opened Heschel's

prophetic imagination and inspired him to be God's companion in prophetic healing. Protesting injustice, Heschel discovered that even his legs were praying. His prayers became incarnation in world-changing social involvement. He became, with Teresa of Avila, the hands and feet of God.

Let my prayers take flight in care for strangers. Let them take legs in protest and presence. Let them take hands in healing touch and loving embrace.

10.

I was suddenly overwhelmed with
the realization that I loved all those people,
that they were mine and I was theirs,
that we could not be alien to one another
even though we were total strangers.
It was like waking from a dream of separateness.

—THOMAS MERTON

Justice emerges from our sense of unity with all creation. Beyond the binary, there is unity. Beyond separation, there is reconciliation.

Despite our differences and unique life experiences and perspectives, we are joined by the grace of interdependence. There is no other. When we look into another's face, we see our own reflection as God's beloved children. Your joy is mine and so is your sorrow. We are kin.

Join us in Your graceful interdependence, Artist of Creation, that we may see each other as kin, embracing each other's joys and sorrows in the quest for wholeness.

11.

This is the day that God has made,
let us rejoice and be glad in it.

—PSALM 118:14

We can be peaceful warriors. We can be joyful activists. We can have enduring joy, even in times of strife, because of our confidence in God's goal of justice. With activist John Lewis, we can make good trouble, knowing the movement of the universe leans toward justice and that our quest for it is rooted in God's wise creativity.

God has made the world and this day, and in this day, we have twenty-four hours to do

something novel, creative, and beautiful. We can rejoice to know that we are seeking—albeit imperfectly—to align ourselves with the everlasting purposes of the universe. This is not to say that we have the audacity to claim that God baptizes our politics; our desire is simply to follow God's path. Even if we appear to fail, we know that God's way will ultimately prevail.

Loving Spirit, let me greet each new day with purpose and joy. Let me do my part to bring beauty to this good Earth. Let my joy resound across my community as I seek to embody Your realm on Earth as it is in Heaven.

12.

Social action, therefore, is an expression of
resistance against whatever tends to,
or separates one, from the experience of God,
who is the ground of [our] being.

—HOWARD THURMAN

Howard Thurman asserted that mysticism leads to social action. Mystics encounter the living God, and from that experience of Divine intimacy, seek to create social conditions that enable everyone to experience that same intimacy. Everything that stands in the way of abundant life is subject to challenge. While mystics challenge perpetrators of injustice, they look for common ground.

When we close our ears to the cries of the poor, we may experience what the prophet Amos describes as a famine of hearing the word of God. "They will wander from sea to sea, and from north to east; they shall run to and fro, seeking the word of God, but they shall not find it" (see Amos 8:10–14). When the soul of the nation is healed through mystic protest, then the sounds of the cities and countryside will be filled with joy and laughter.

Let my faith take shape in acts of justice and mercy. Let my encounter with You, Spirit, open my senses to the tragic beauty of life and let me hear the pain of the world and respond with lovingkindness, seeking justice and peace for all.

13.

He comes to us as One unknown,
without a name . . .
and sets us to the tasks
which He has to fulfill for our time. . . .
He will reveal Himself in the toils,
the conflicts, the sufferings
which they shall pass through
in His fellowship,
and, as an ineffable mystery,
they shall learn in their own
experience Who He is.

—ALBERT SCHWEITZER

God's vision is always more than we can imagine. God gives us a dream and invites us to follow. We may not fully know the One who calls or that One's intentions, but in the adventure of companionship, we discover who we are and what God wants of us. The mysteries of life are always beyond our comprehension but in the pilgrimage toward just peace and healing, the veil is lifted, and we glimpse God in the challenges, celebrations, and conflicts of each new day. Revelation is right where we are. Insight emerges on the journey.

Loving Mystery, I do not claim to know You nor can I control Your presence in the world—but I seek to follow Your vision.

14.

During my most difficult moments
and complex situations I have been
able to dream of a more beautiful future.

—RIGOBERTA MENCHU

Described as an indigenous feminist and human rights activist, Rigoberta Menchu reminds us that visualizing alternative realities to the current injustice is essential to peacemaking and justice-seeking. The ability to imagine a different world, governed by different values, energized Menchu's work in her homeland Guatemala and her advocacy for indigenous peoples across the globe.

Our current personal, political, or economic situation need not imprison us. Prophetic dreamers soar on eagle's wings far beyond the injustices they experience. They envision pathways to freedom and full humanity for all God's children. They see the wealthy learning to care and the oppressed shaping their futures. The present moment is the womb of possibility and the birthplace of dreams.

Loving Spirit, give me big dreams. Let my dreams inspire action. Empower me to take my place as Your companion on the pathway to Shalom.

15.

Every one of us can make a contribution.
And quite often we are looking for
the big things and forget that,
wherever we are, we can make a contribution.
Sometimes I tell myself, I may only
be planting a tree here,
but just imagine what's happening
if there are billions of people
out there doing something.
Just imagine the power of what we can do.

—WANGARI MAATHAI

Kenyan social, environmental, and political activist and the first African woman to win the Nobel Peace Prize, Wangari Maathai started a movement that has planted over 30 million trees in response to deforestation in her native Africa. She recognizes that individually our contributions may seem insignificant. But, like the mustard seed of Jesus' parable, when we join with others in devotion to purposes greater than self-interest, the world is transformed. As Robert Schuller once said, we can count the seeds in an apple but not the apples in a seed. The world is saved one person and one sacrifice at a time.

God of apple seeds and mustard plants, thank You for giving me a vision of possibilities.

16.

Never believe that a few caring people
can't change the world.
That's all who ever have.

—MARGARET MEAD

As the story goes, Jesus had just finished preaching to a crowd of several thousand people. Now it was growing late, and the people were hungry. Jesus called out for people to share their lunches. Only a child came forward—but Jesus saw a vast feast in a child's meal. While I believe that Jesus' embodiment of the Energy of Love can produce miracles using the powers inherent in the natural world, perhaps a greater miracle

occurred when members of the crowd observed the boy's generosity, pulled out their knapsacks, and shared with their neighbors.

A few friends, a few loaves and fish—a small group can change a community and be the catalyst for global transformation. What is God calling us to do?

Spirit of Infinite Possibility, give me a glimpse of greatness in small things, in change emerging from a new perspective, in healing coming from a few joined hands. Let me claim my agency and discover companions with whom I can dedicate my energy and talents for peace and justice.

17.

Let the words of my mouth
and meditation of my heart
be acceptable in your sight,
O God, my rock and redeemer.

—PSALM 19:14

Character matters. Words matter. Truth matters. Denial and falsehood lead to death and destruction, while truth enables us to respond creatively to life's crises.

Justice-seekers commit themselves to honesty and factuality at every level. They work to deepen their spiritual lives as the foundation for politics

that heal rather than divide. Healthy transformation comes from the hard work of spiritual growth and courageous reconciliation, while still refusing to accept injustice. Although we confront intolerance and prejudice, we do so with civility and respect. We seek to heal oppressor and oppressed alike. We are challenged to see the Divine in those whom we challenge.

Healing Spirit, give us courage and strength to confront evil. Let our inner work inspire just reconciliation with those who perpetrate injustice.

18.

Because blacks so profoundly symbolize
race in the white consciousness,
any white person who wants to challenge racism
and engage in antiracist practice
must work to specifically address
the messages they have internalized
about black people.

—ROBIN DIANGELO

The Ignatian Examen has found a place at the heart of Christian spirituality. It involves looking at our lives without blinders, and we can use this mindfulness process to become more aware of our attitudes toward issues of race, economics,

and sexuality. Given the realities of structural racism and inherited racist attitudes, those of us who are white need to explore our conscious and unconscious attitudes toward persons of color. This can be painful, but to be an anti-racist, we must commit ourselves to being self-aware, to challenging implicit racism, and working toward just economic and judicial structures, transforming our nation's "original sins" of slavery, racism, and genocide of indigenous peoples.

God of All Peoples, let me embrace the world in all its diversity. Let me stand with those who suffer structural injustice and work toward liberty and justice for all Your children.

19.

Like anybody, I would like to live. . . .
But I'm not concerned about that now.
I just want to do God's will.
And He's allowed me to go up to the mountain. . . .
And I've seen the Promised Land. . . .
I'm not worried about anything.
I'm not fearing any man.
Mine eyes have seen the glory
of the coming of the Lord.

—MARTIN LUTHER KING JR.

On April 3, 1968, Martin Luther King Jr. spoke about the Promised Land of justice and freedom. The next day he was assassinated—but from the mountaintop, he had received a God's-eye view of history, of what the world will look like when we make a commitment to bring the Divine vision to Earth.

We too have seen the Promised Land, and yet the forces of fear and hate seek to bar the way. We cannot give up. We must push forward toward horizons of hope for all God's children.

Guide me one step at a time, Spirit, by the call of liberty and justice for all.

20.

> Revolution is not a one-time event.
> —AUDRE LORDE

Self-described "black, lesbian, mother, warrior, poet," Audre Lorde dedicated her life to confronting injustice, homophobia, sexism, and racism. She knew that the far horizons of justice are constantly receding. We must keep moving forward, aiming toward the Promised Land God imagines for humankind in its diversity.

Spirituality is revolutionary. It challenges the present in light of the future God imagines for us. The backward-looking conservative, content with

the old-time religion or an idealized past, goes against the nature of God's evolving universe. Behold, God is doing a new thing. God's new creation lures us forward, challenging us to be revolutionaries of spirituality and relationships.

Loving Spirit, help me be a champion of Your compassionate revolution. Let me join calm with restlessness and peace with action to embody Your heavenly vision in my life and in the world.

21.

I was taught to see racism only as individual acts of meanness, not in invisible systems conferring dominance on my group.

—PEGGY MCINTOSH

Peggy McIntosh, who, along with David Wellman, originated the term "white privilege," states that white privilege is "an invisible package of unearned assets that I can count on cashing in each day, but about which I was 'meant' to remain oblivious. White privilege is like an invisible weightless knapsack of special provisions, assurances, tools, maps, guides, codebooks, passports, visas, clothes, compass, emergency gear, and blank checks."

The mindfulness that is necessary for spiritual growth challenges us to recognize the advantages we have based on race. We need to see where our privilege connects with the suffering of others. We need to recognize our complicity in structural and economic racism and discrimination. Those of us who are white need to be aware of our inherent privilege, not with guilt or shame, but as inspiration to creative transformation. Spiritual mindfulness challenges us to share our privilege with others and work for a work of equality and justice for all people.

Wake me up, Spirit, to the privileges I have that harm others. Wake me up to the need for justice for all Your children.

22.

We will have to repent in this generation
not merely for the hateful words and
actions of the bad people
but for the appalling silence of the good people.

—MARTIN LUTHER KING JR.

The denigration of marginalized people, especially persons of color, LGBTQ persons, and immigrants, occurs in many forms. We know the dangers of hate speech and racist behaviors, but there is another danger: keeping silent when others suffer from injustice, socially or individually. We cannot afford to ignore the pain others experience when they are maligned.

We need to repent, turning from apathy to empathy and empathy to agency for the well-being of all. We need to be allies of all who suffer injustice. Our presence creates a circle of protection around those whom we honor as our siblings. And then, if we can spiritually connect with the aggressor as well, our presence can be the first step toward reconciliation.

Spirit of Love and Justice, inspire me to stand beside all those who suffer injustice. Give me courage to speak for the silenced and honor outsiders as Your beloved children.

23.

> I am not free while any woman is unfree,
> even if her shackles
> are very different from my own.
>
> —AUDRE LORDE

The glass ceiling in professional and political life has stifled women's imaginations. Now the ceiling is being broken and new possibilities are emerging for women as well as the LGBTQ and the African American communities. As I write these words, Senator Kamala Harris has been chosen as Vice President-elect, the first woman to hold this role. Young girls of all colors are seeing themselves in her election.

Justice-seekers and peacemakers must become allies of everyone who is dispossessed, marginalized, or limited by our culture and social structures. While letting go of paternalism, men—most especially white, heterosexual, cisgender men—must see advocacy for those who have experienced sexism as our soul work in the twenty-first century. Letting go of privilege and being willing to change our behaviors, we can be companions in a world where diversity in all its wonder is honored and affirmed.

Spirit, help me to repent of sexism and commit myself to a spirituality of justice-seeking. Let the circle of justice begin with me and radiate to embrace all Your children.

24.

I am not afraid; I was born to do this.

—JOAN OF ARC

In the film *Chariots of Fire*, Olympic medalist Eric Liddell responds to his sister's worries that focusing on running will deter him from going to the missionary field with the words, "I believe God made me for a purpose. God made me fast and when I run, I feel his pleasure." Liddell was called to be a runner. He was also called to be a missionary in China and died in a Japanese internment camp in 1945. He knew his vocation and so did Saint Joan, who felt God's call to liberate the French people.

When we know our calling, we can go forward with courage and love. We face challenges, believing that God walks beside us, guiding, protecting, and welcoming us into the eternal realm at the moment of death. Regardless of our age, God has a vision for our lives. It isn't predetermined. It is an offering of graceful possibility awaiting our decisions. In saying "yes," to God's dream for our lives, we awaken to new power, love, and creativity. We become part of a larger journey, where all are pilgrims, and none are strangers.

Thank You, Loving Spirit, for having a vision—and possibilities—for my life and for this moment.

25.

Because you are alive, everything is possible.

—THICH NHAT HANH

These days many of us feel disempowered. Even people with privilege wonder if they have any impact on our nation's institutions and political decision-making. In success or failure, however, we each awakened today to a plethora of possibilities. Each moment presents us with options for choosing our adventures as God's beloved children. We are seldom without the resources to reach out, embrace another person, and take our place on the side of the angels.

We are alive and we can make choices. We can be agents of destiny. We can pray for guidance and discover the wisdom of the spiritual, "This little light of mine, I'm gonna let it shine," casting out chaos and confusion, hatred and contempt, and being a witness for God's love in a broken world.

I thank You, Spirit, for waking me up to possibility and the opportunity to do something beautiful for You and the world.

26.

I was hungry and you gave me food,
I was thirsty and you gave me
something to drink,
I was a stranger and you welcomed me,
I was naked and you gave me clothing,
I was sick and you took care of me,
I was in prison and you visited me....
As you did it to one of the least of these
who are members of my family, you did it to me.

—MATTHEW 25: 34–36, 44

God feels the hopelessness of asylum seekers and children separated from their parents on the US border. God experiences the terror of a young black man being choked to death by law officers or the grief of a young woman's family following her unwarranted death in a police shootout. God is the Open Heart of the Universe.

In many Benedictine monasteries, you may see a plaque that counsels, "Treat everyone as Christ." Christ comes to us, as Mother Teresa of Calcutta averred, in distressing disguises. How we treat others is how we treat Christ.

Spirit, let me see Your face in everyone.

27.

> The Bible directs [us]
> to God's powerlessness and suffering;
> only the suffering God can help.
>
> —DIETRICH BONHOEFFER

Writing from a Nazi prison, young theologian-pastor Dietrich Bonhoeffer experienced God as his intimate companion. God is where the pain is. God is where the joy is. In suffering with us, God heals our wounds and gives us strength and vision for the journey ahead.

As the song of my childhood says, "What a friend we have in Jesus, all our sins and griefs to bear. What a privilege to carry everything to God in prayer." Our quest for justice and peace in a world of conflict mirrors God's quest, and our commitment to God's way brings joy to God's heart and to our fellow creatures. Not aloof, God is where the suffering is.

Heart of the Universe, let my heart beat with Yours. Let me feel Your pain at the world's suffering. Let me feel Your companionship as I seek to follow Your way. Help me to bring healing balm to suffering people by acts of kindness and justice-seeking.

28.

When I say it's you I like, I'm talking about that part of you that knows that life is far more than anything you can ever see or hear or touch. That deep part of you that allows you to stand for those things without which humankind cannot survive. Love that conquers hate, peace that rises triumphant over war, and justice that proves more powerful than greed.

—FRED ROGERS

Fred Rogers was a shaman of the Spirit for millions of children, helping them realize their inner resources and Divine destiny. You may be a shaman of the Spirit for a child or someone injured by the world's injustice. Your love can liberate and transform, awakening holiness where it lies hidden.

Spirit of Transformation, inspire me to be Your shaman, an agent of liberation in large and small situations, bringing forth beauty where it lies hidden and love where it has been lost.

29.

> You don't make progress by standing on the sidelines, whimpering and complaining.
> You make progress by implementing ideas.
>
> —SHIRLEY CHISHOLM

Shirley Chisholm, the first African American woman elected to Congress, knew what it was like to move from the sidelines to the frontlines of American politics. Due to economic stress in her family, Shirley, aged five, and her two sisters were sent to live with her grandmother in Barbados. Being with an elder was a godsend for Shirley. "Granny gave me strength, dignity, and

love. I learned from an early age that I was somebody," Shirley recalled. Despite opposition due to her gender, as an adult, Shirley Chisholm got involved in politics and was elected to Congress and later was the first African American to run for President of the United States. She recognized that we need to transform our complaints and excuses into activism. We need to move from passivity to agency and claim our role as agents of peace, freedom, and justice, despite the obstacles that others put in our way.

Push me, Divine Spirit, out from the sidelines into the frontlines. Deliver me from passivity. Challenge me to agency and empathy.

30.

Learn to be quiet enough to hear
the genuine within yourself
so that you can hear it in others.

—MARIAN WRIGHT EDELMAN

Founder of the Children's Defense Fund, Marian Wright Edelman invites us to take time for stillness. Stillness opens us to our deeper wisdom. Pausing awhile to listen to our lives awakens us to the fullness of our experience. We learn to befriend the shadow as well as the light, the calm as well as the restlessness, the love as well as the hate. In knowing ourselves and being quiet

enough to embrace the breadth of our experience, we open our hearts to hearing the experiences of others.

With nothing to hide or defend, we can listen to others' experiences without judgment or condemnation. Silence enables us to experience contrasting viewpoints without polarization, challenge without hatred, and criticism without defensiveness. Steeped in the deep peace of self-awareness, we can face conflict with confidence and wisdom, knowing we have spiritual resources to weather the storms of social upheaval.

Loving Spirit, let the deep peace of the universe be mine. Let the breadth of self-awareness be mine. Let confidence and connection in times of trial be mine.

31.

Struggle is a never ending process.
Freedom is never really won,
you earn it and win it in every generation.

—CORETTA SCOTT KING

There is a prophetic restlessness in life. The prophet experiences a faithful discontent with the world as it is. No political system or leader perfectly embodies God's vision. Nor does any politician or policy deserve our ultimate loyalty.

Will we further the moral arc of history or will we stand in the way of God's quest for justice? Will we preserve or expand hard-fought gains in human rights, or will we complacently allow

the forces of intolerance and oppression to gain the upper hand? Each day is an opportunity to expand the circle of justice. Each decision moves our world closer or further from God's dream of Shalom. Blacksliding is always a threat. Human rights and political self-determination are always under attack from the forces of prejudice, intolerance, and oppression. Keep alert, keep awake, keep active.

Give me, Spirit of Shalom, prophetic restlessness. Deliver me from complacency. Let me not take for granted the stony road toward justice.

32.

Every great dream begins with a dreamer.

—HARRIET TUBMAN

Harriett Tubman was inspired by the dream of freedom. Dreaming of freedom, however, isn't enough. Her dreams inspired her own flight to freedom, and then she went on thirteen missions, guiding another seventy-one slaves to freedom. For Tubman, the dream took her beyond individual freedom and led her to become an abolitionist and crusader for women's suffrage.

We need great dreams today. We need to awaken to God's dream of Shalom for our planet

as well as God's dream for ourselves. God's dream embraces environmental, economic, and racial justice. It inspires us to leave our comfort zones to explore the frontiers of spiritual growth and political activism.

What is your great dream? What great personal and planetary work does your dream inspire? Greatness comes in many forms. But it begins with a dream and a dreamer, and the dreamer is you!

Loving Spirit, give me a great dream and the energy to embody it in my daily life and politics. Let me experience Your dream for the Earth and its peoples as my polestar and inspiration.

33.

Deep listening is the kind of listening
that can help relieve the suffering
of another person.

—THICH NHAT HANH

This morning as I walked along the Cape Cod beach near my home, I encountered a woman walking in my direction. She appeared to stiffen and become more vigilant and distanced herself from me by a few paces. Perhaps it was COVID concerns, although I had my mask on. It might also have been concern about my presence as a male, since we were the only ones on the beach at sunrise. Given the realities of assault, she had reason to be a little nervous. If she had been

concerned about a stranger on the beach, I could not change her feelings, but I could honor her distancing and try to relieve her concerns by my benign behavior. Some of my African American friends tell me that they find it difficult to trust white people, given that half voted for a candidate known for racism in the 2020 presidential election. White people must be aware of African Americans' anxiety around us. Despite our perceived innocence, we need to honor others' fears and prayerfully do our best to respond with grace, understanding, and assurance. The way to peace may come one smile at a time.

Loving Spirit, help me be a sign of peace, safety, and acceptance, willing to go beyond my own defensiveness to respond to the pain others feel.

34.

I will remove from your body the heart
of stone and give you a heart of flesh.

—EZEKIEL 36:26

The prophet Ezekiel is prescribing spiritual open-heart surgery. His nation had closed its heart to God's vision and to the cries of the poor. They had focused on possessions and power and protecting their privilege. They had forgotten the needy and vulnerable and put their ease ahead of their children's future. They were in need of heart transformation.

A heart of flesh is a strong, open, empathetic heart. A heart that beats in sync with the heartbeat of God. A heart that feels pain and joy and recognizes its own rhythm in every life. Let us have a new heart, not just as individuals, but as nations. Let us privilege the poor. Embrace the immigrant. Cherish the child. May we have new hearts so we can feel our connection with the Earth in all its wondrous beauty, amazing diversity, and painful brokenness.

Heart of Creation, give me a new heart. Let my heart beat in sync with Yours. Let me hear the heartbeat of creation and feel the life we all share course through my veins.

35.

> Progress is founded upon the experience of discordant feelings. The social value of liberty lies in its production of discords.
>
> —ALFRED NORTH WHITEHEAD

Conflict can be creative. Difference can bring change. Some of the most important growth occurs when we recognize the difference between where we currently are and where God wants us to be. God is the source of loving discord as well as healing calm. The framers of the American Constitution spoke of a "more perfect union," recognizing that we had a long way to go as a nation. That spirit, inherent in the quest for a more perfect union with liberty for justice for all,

drove our nation forward, inspiring prayers and protests to abolish slavery, give women voting rights, seek equality in the economy and the polling booth for persons of color, protect the rights of the LGBTQ community, and promote Earth care. Among loving hearts and welcoming minds, discord is transformative. Discord wakes us up to injustice and inspires us to heal the soul of the nation. Discord gives life to dead souls, energy to the apathetic, and hope to the forgotten. As Robert Kennedy said, "Some men see things as they are, and ask why. I dream of things that never were, and ask why not."

Spirit of New Creation, let the discord between what is and what could be inspire me toward ever-expanding harmonies of hospitality and circles of care.

36.

The pure conservative is going against the essence of the universe.

—ALFRED NORTH WHITEHEAD

The philosopher Whitehead noted that the aim of life is first to live, then to live well, and finally to live better. The evolutionary processes that brought forth the galaxies, solar systems, and planets, and then moved toward the creation of more complex living beings, such as ourselves, are at work in our moral lives. While the evolution of morality is tenuous at best, it is always forward-looking. There is no perfect paradise to go back to. There is no ideal in national history beckoning us backward. History moves forward, and our calling is to shape the contours of our communities,

in all their emerging diversity and creativity, in ways that promote abundant living for all.

We can't go back to the 1950s. The good old days may not have been so good—for indigenous people, persons of color, LGBTQ folk, and women seeking equality. The placid days of Christian and white exceptionalism were also days of McCarthyism, separate but equal, living in the closet, and women restricted to homelife. God's Shalom always drives us forward. Justice beckons us to new horizons. With insight and integrity, let us move forward, honoring the past and reaching toward new moral and spiritual horizons.

Spirit of discord and harmony, protest and reconciliation, join me with others around the common cause of national and personal healing, so that the bells of liberty and justice might ring out for all people.

37.

Save us from weak resignation
to the evils we deplore;
let the gift of your salvation
be our glory evermore.

—HARRY EMERSON FOSDICK

It is easy to give up hope, especially when it comes to bringing justice to the world. Sometimes we are inclined to believe that the best we can hope for is putting our finger in the dike, holding back the waters of racism, incivility, injustice, and ecocide. Yet, to move forward, we need to believe that change can occur, and we can be part of it.

In this time of COVID-19, many of our external options have been circumscribed. We are wary of public gatherings and protests, going to in-person meetings, and doing our usual volunteer activities. Yet we can still do something. We can call our representatives, challenging them to do more for justice and Earth care. We can make a donation to the food pantry, soup kitchen, or a nonprofit group that supports justice, peace, and environmental healing. We can be God's hands and feet.

Spirit, let my light shine in the darkness of greed and injustice, revealing and healing one moment and situation at a time.

38.

The greatest challenge of the day is:
how to bring about a revolution of the heart,
a revolution that has to start with each one of us?

—DOROTHY DAY

John the Baptist challenged his hearers to repent and change their lives. Repentance means to turn around, go in a new direction, and change our lives. A revolution in the heart orients us in an entirely new direction, moving from self-interest to loving our neighbor with the same concern as we love ourselves. Dorothy Day answered her question, saying, "When we begin to take the lowest place, to wash the feet of

others, to love our brothers with that burning love, that passion, which led to the Cross, then we can truly say, 'Now I have begun.'"

In the spirit of Jesus, greatness is found in servanthood and mission. We commit ourselves to service, to bringing joy and hope to every situation. To letting go of privilege so others can lead. To living more simply to ensure the survival of our vulnerable neighbors and the planet. We need a new orientation, a revolution of the heart that begins with our own personal transformation and spirals out to embrace larger and larger circles of love.

Spirit of Transformation, help me to let my world revolve around others' well-being and not my desires alone.

39.

> To be patient and kind, that was
> the philosophy I have adopted after the attack.
>
> —MALALA YOUSAFZAI

In 2012, gunmen boarded a bus, identified fifteen-year-old Malala Yousafzai, and shot her in the forehead, in reprisal for her speaking out for the rights of Pakistani girls. Malala survived to become a human rights advocate and the youngest person to win the Nobel Peace Prize. The attack and painful healing process that followed could have embittered Malala. Her world could have shrunk to the size of her anger and griev-

ance. Instead, her spirit soared and expanded. She grew in wisdom and stature. She discovered that love and mercy are pathways to personal and political liberation. She chose not to harbor anger but focus on love.

Deep down, everyone—even the gun-toting vigilante, the Taliban revolutionary, the bloviating politician, the knee-jerk racist—cries out for patience and love, for understanding and compassion. We can heal the world through ever-expanding circles of love and forgiveness.

Spirit of All Creation, as You have loved me, let me love others. As You have forgiven me, let me forgive others. Let me seek reconciliation, grounded in loving power, with those who oppose the quest for peace and justice.

40.

A person with ubuntu is open and available
to others, affirming of others, does not feel
threatened that others are able and good,
for he or she has a proper self-assurance that
comes from knowing that he or she belongs
in a greater whole and is diminished
when others are humiliated or diminished,
when others are tortured or oppressed, or
treated as if they were less than who they are.

—DESMOND TUTU

The Southern Africa word *ubuntu* proclaims that "I am because of you." We live in a world of intricate and dynamic interdependence in which everyone matters. We are not separate but part of a living body, the "body of Christ," as the Apostle Paul affirms, or the "net of Indra" as Buddhist teachers affirm. When we go beyond the illusion of separate selfhood and binary win-lose, in-out thinking, we realize that our joys and sorrow are one. When opened to the spirit of ubuntu, our souls expand and range across the universe.

Awaken me, Spirit, to the wondrous joy of interdependence.

41.

What we need to discover in the social realm
is the moral equivalent of war:
something heroic that will speak to men
as universally as war does.
And yet will be as compatible with their
spiritual selves as war has proved incompatible.

—WILLIAM JAMES

We need a new kind of patriotism for today's interdependent world. We need to elicit a new kind of passion, "the moral equivalent of war" as

philosopher-psychologist William James asserts, in which we expand our loyalties from self-interest, community, and nation, to planetary. Our future is at stake as much as it was in World War II. We need to come together, let go of individual greed, and sacrifice for the greater good of future generations and the planet. We need to say a resounding "yes," when our grandchildren ask, "Did you fight to save the soul of our nation? Did you fight for justice? Did you fight for the planet?"

Let me, O Spirit, feel Your passion for peace, justice, and planetary healing.

42.

Not one of us can rest,
be happy, be at home,
be at peace with ourselves,
until we end hatred and division.

—JOHN LEWIS

"Let there be peace on earth and let it begin with me," the singer chants. Peace is an inner journey. A commitment to healing and wholeness. A willingness to examine our lives, challenge our assumptions, and look beyond self-interest and ego gratification. Peace begins with embracing

the deep peace of God and trusting our lives to a Wisdom and Power greater than our own.

Peace is also an outer journey. Our inner quest must be joined with an outer commitment to create institutions of peace and justice that enable others to experience peace and wholeness. Shalom is not accidental. It is the result of peace-seeking people banding together to create a peaceful society and a healthy planet. Without inner peace, there cannot be outer peace, and without outer peace, the quest for inner peace and wholeness becomes insurmountable.

Let the circles of peace radiate from my life, Spirit, to include other peacemakers, joined in common cause, and stretched across the Earth.

43.

Do not be anxious about anything,
but in every situation, by prayer and petition,
with thanksgiving, present your requests
to God. And the peace of God,
which transcends all understanding,
will guard your hearts
and your minds in Christ Jesus.

—PHILIPPIANS 4:4–7

These days we need to guard our hearts. There is much that makes us anxious—pandemic, climate change, systemic injustice, demagogic politicians, and the rise of white nationalism.

As we confront these threats to our nation's and planet's future, we need to be grounded in God's peace. Peace emerges from a lively, intimate relationship with God in which our lives become a sustained conversation with the One to whom all hearts are open and all desires known. Recognizing the gifts of life, we can come to God with our deepest needs, knowing that we are never alone, and that God constantly provides us with resources to seek healing in our relationships and political involvement.

Spirit, may Your peace give me calm confidence in Your providence supporting my role in healing my community and the nation.

44.

When I liberate myself, I liberate others.
If you don't speak out
ain't nobody going to speak out for you.

—FANNY LOU HAMER

Civil and women's rights activist Fanny Lou Hamer knew that when we refuse to accept the limits others place on us, we enable others to find personal freedom. Like Martin Luther King Jr. and John Lewis, Hamer experienced the violence of "law and order," meted out by racist social structures. Despite the risk, she knew that when someone speaks their truth, God makes a way for countless other justice-seekers.

Many of us are victims of our own self-imposed limitations. We have erected prisons of the spirit that prevent us from realizing God's dream for our lives. Liberation involves both personal and social transformation. If we remain silent, we jeopardize the lives of persons of color, indigenous people, asylum seekers, and members of the LGBTQ community. Listen for God's voice, inspiring your voice, and then let your life speak.

Thank You, Spirit, for giving me models of just peacemakers. May I walk in their footsteps.

45.

Lord Jesus Christ,
have mercy upon me, a sinner.

—"THE JESUS PRAYER"

There are powers within us and in the world that threaten to undermine our confidence and self-esteem. We feel alone, incompetent, and without resources to face today's personal and political challenges. Placing our weakness and fear in God's hands, however, gives us courage and confidence far beyond what we can ask or imagine. In our brokenness, we find healing. In

our loneliness, we find companions. In our sin, we experience mercy. Casting our lives on God's mercy, we open the floodgates of Divine possibility. Doors open. Power bursts forth. Courage empowers. And we will renew our strength, mount up with wings like eagles, run and not be weary, and walk and not faint (Isaiah 40:31).

Spirit, give me strength in my weakness, love in my enmity, trust in my fear, and energy in my weariness. Let Your power course through me, giving life and light to the world.

46.

Never forget that justice is
what love looks like in public.

—CORNEL WEST

Social activists remind us that the personal is the political and the political is the personal. Public policy is never abstract and unrelated to the lives of people. Political decisions are always concrete and can be a matter of life and death for millions of people. There is only one world, and that's God's world. God's realm is intended to be here on Earth, not postponed to the afterlife.

Many people who are loving in their one-to-one relationships support policies that harm children, disenfranchise persons of color, and promote incivility in the political arena. In contrast, God's way joins the inner and outer and the personal and political. God invites us to embody a politics of compassion—love in action.

Spirit, let love guide my relationships, my political involvement, and my involvement in my community. Let the love I have for my neighbors expand to embrace social justice and care for all Your creation.

47.

We say no to the peace that keeps us on our
knees, no to the peace that keeps us in chains,
no to the false peace that denies
the values and contributions of our peoples.

—RIGOBERTA MENCHU

There is the false peace of "law and order," when troops line the city streets, call curfews, and stifle dissent. There is the false peace of quiet city streets that hide families cowering in their homes, fearful of reprisal from vigilantes, demagogues, and dictators. But there can be no true

peace without justice. Peace is the harmony of many voices in sync, sharing a hymn that takes them from self-interest to symphony. A harmony in which every voice is heard, every talent is supported, and diversity is embraced as a gift.

Loving Spirit, let me listen to the many songs of life. Let there be Bach and hip-hop, jazz and Pachelbel, swing and blues, gospel and Gaelic. Let all creation sing a chorus of peace.

48.

I am stronger than fear.

—MALALA YOUSAFZAI

It has been said that courage is fear that has said its prayers. Prayer connects us with the creative power of the universe that will outlast any foe. Prayer reminds us that "nothing can separate us from the love of God" (Romans 8:38). Every justice-seeker may have to face conflict and threat when we challenge racist, homophobic, or sexist remarks. We may not face terrorism, as Malala did, but we may lose friends. We may feel awkward. Our fear may still paralyze us and

prevent us from doing the work of justice to which God calls us.

But we are stronger than our fears. God is stronger than our worry or conflict avoidance. If we take our concerns to God, we will receive guidance and confidence that even in our fears, God is with us.

Holy One, inspire me to pray my fears and trust Your presence as I venture faithfully and lovingly to support the forgotten, oppressed, and marginalized. Let me risk speaking up when silence seems convenient, knowing that in my speaking, I take my place as Your companion in bringing healing to the dispossessed.

49.

You can't separate peace from freedom
because no one can be at peace
unless he has his freedom.

—MALCOLM X

African American social activist and justice-seeker Malcolm X evolved from focusing his message primarily on the black community to becoming an activist for global justice. His life was transformed when he visited Mecca, where he had a chance to share his beliefs with other cultures and affirm the gifts of white and black people alike. He reported meeting "blonde-haired,

blue-eyed men I could call my brothers." Sadly, his life was cut short by an assassin's bullet as he was beginning a new path in racial reconciliation.

Peacemakers expand freedom and creativity congruent with the well-being of the whole. Healthy societies encourage creativity and challenge. Healthy justice-seeking aims at the creation of relationships that enhance creativity and agency.

Spirit of Prophetic Healing, let Your healing power inspire me to promote the creativity and agency of others, especially the vulnerable and marginalized. Let me be willing to hear their protests prayerfully and without defensiveness, going beyond my self-interest to promote Your Beloved Community.

50.

Never be afraid to make some noise,
and get in good trouble, necessary trouble.

—JOHN LEWIS

Deeply spiritual, John Lewis knew what it was like to both pray and protest. Beaten at Selma, Alabama, on the Pettus Bridge, Lewis put his life on the line to achieve justice for African Americans. He continued to pray and protest throughout his career as a Congressman. Just a few days before his death, Lewis sent a piece to the *New York Times*, his final public message, addressed to justice-seekers and peacemakers

everywhere: "Though I may not be here with you, I urge you to answer the highest calling of your heart and stand up for what you truly believe. In my life, I have done all I can to demonstrate that the way of peace, the way of love and nonviolence is the more excellent way. Now it is your turn to let freedom ring. . . . So I say to you, walk with the wind, brothers and sisters, and let the spirit of peace and the power of everlasting love be your guide."

Let me be willing, Spirit of Restless Justice-Seeking, to make good trouble to embody Your realm of Shalom on Earth as it is in Heaven.

51.

Faith by itself, without works, is dead...
faith was brought to completion by the works.

—JAMES 2:17, 22

Authentic spirituality joins our personal relationship with God and our care for our neighbor. We can't claim to love God if we don't respond to the food insecurity or homelessness of our community. We can't claim to affirm family values if we condone separating children from their parents on the US borderlands or oppose the funding of food programs for young children. Authentic

faith is relational and holistic, not a transaction between God and ourselves as individuals. The grace we've received inspires grace to our neighbor and a politics of grace that seeks to uplift all humankind. As the Dalai Lama asserts, "My religion is kindness," kindness that encompasses the State House as well as our neighbor's house.

Out of the love I have received from You, Spirit, let me love my neighbor and make a commitment to love in action in my personal relationships and public policy advocacy.

52.

Blessed are those who hunger and thirst for righteousness, for they will be filled.

—MATTHEW 5:6

The questions are often asked, "How badly do you want to change your life? How important is changing the world to you?" Or, as theologian Paul Tillich queried, what is your ultimate concern and what are you going to do about it? Jesus talked about a yearning—a hunger and thirst—for wholeness. The righteous ones are committed to their own spiritual growth and purity of heart and personal behavior—and they also recognize that they must be equally commit-

ted to righteousness in public policy. Our moral commitments must take us beyond the personal to the political as we seek a world of justice supporting the growth of all God's children. The question remains—and this is a question asked by our grandchildren and the daughter of George Floyd—"How committed are you to our future? Do you thirst for justice? Do you hunger for ecological healing?"

Holy One, stir my passion for justice. Let me hunger and thirst for safe streets for children, voting rights for adults, healthy environments for families, jobs that promote dignity, food enough for all, and hospitality to strangers.

53.

Blessed are the merciful,
for they will receive mercy.

—MATTHEW 5:7

William Shakespeare asserts that "the quality of mercy is not strained. It droppeth as the gentle rain from heaven Upon the place beneath. It is twice blessed: It blesseth him that gives and him that takes." The bard continues that mercy is "an attribute to God." Mercy expresses our compassion and empathy, our attempt to understand and reach out, to those who may have threatened us. It extends the olive branch of peace. It seeks reconciliation.

At the end of the Civil War, President Abraham Lincoln was asked how he would treat the Southern states. Despite their treasonous behavior, Lincoln replied, "I would treat them as if they never left." In his second inaugural speech, Lincoln embodied the quality of mercy toward those who had been defeated: "With malice toward none, with charity for all, with firmness in the right as God gives us to see the right, let us strive on to finish the work we are in, to bind up the nation's wounds, to care for him who shall have borne the battle and for his widow and his orphan, to do all which may achieve and cherish a just and lasting peace among ourselves and with all nations." Let the spirit of mercy expand in our own turbulent time.

Let us be strong about our calling to be peacemakers and justice-seekers, O Spirit—but let us also be merciful and compassionate, expanding the circle of love to include friend and foe alike.

54.

Blessed are the peacemakers,
for they will be called children of God.

—MATTHEW 5:9

Despite the conflicts in the world, Judaism, Christianity, and Islam see God as the God of Peace. God's Shalom is the goal of history. God's movements in history are aimed at a time in which swords will be beaten into plowshares, and the lion and the lamb will play together in the Peaceable Realm.

Peacemakers are in sync with God's vision of Shalom. God's ideals inspire and energize them, emerging from the inner calm and expanding into outward acts of reconciliation. When we seek peace, we truly experience ourselves as God's children, revealing God's vision in space and time.

Spirit of Grace and Glory, bless me with Your peace and inspire me to be Your companion, Your hands and feet, as a peacemaker in a world of conflict.

55.

You have heard that it was said,
"You should love your neighbor
and hate your enemy."
But I say to you, Love your neighbors
and pray for those who persecute you,
so that you may be children
of your Parent in heaven;
for God makes the sun
to rise on the evil and the good,
and sends rain on the righteous and unrighteous.

—MATTHEW 5:43-45

God is, as St. Bonaventure said, the circle whose center is everywhere and whose circumference is nowhere. Everyone is at the center of God's love, and God's love includes everyone. Hate creates an infinite chasm. Love brings hope of healing. Hate builds walls. Love builds bridges. Poet Edwin Markham once wrote: "He drew a circle that shut me out— Rebel, heretic, thing to flout. But love and I had the wit to win: We drew a circle that took him in."

Loving Spirit, help me be a circle drawer and love finder, a companion to all Your children.

56.

Abstaining from false speech,
abstaining from malicious speech,
abstaining from harsh speech,
and abstaining from idle chatter
—this is called right speech.

—GUATAMA BUDDHA

The psalmist counseled: "Let the words of my mouth and meditation of my heart be acceptable in thy sight." Gautama Buddha emphasized the centrality of speaking with honesty, compassion, and insight. The words we speak shape

reality. Words can cure; they can also kill. Buddha recognized that right speech is essential to spiritual growth. Do we speak words of love? Do we focus on facts and not fantasies? Do our words affirm the value of others and promote community? Do our words reconcile and upbuild diverse groups? Every word can be healing. Every word can create beauty. Every word can be a prayer.

Loving Spirit, let my words heal, reconcile, and upbuild. Let me speak honestly and lovingly, and may each word be a gift to You.

57.

One is mindful to abandon wrong action
and to enter and remain in right action:
This is one's right mindfulness.
Thus these three qualities—
right view, right effort, and right mindfulness—
run and circle around right action.

—GAUTAMA BUDDHA

Our actions matter. They can create environments that promote healing and creativity. In an interdependent world, even the smallest

actions can transform the world. Small actions done over and over again lead to great changes in character. Changes in character lead to changes in our environment. Acts of love heal. Acts of compassion create community. Every moment matters and everyone matters. The world is healed one moment and action at a time.

Let my every action be prayerful, Spirit. Let me devote my actions to Your vision of Shalom one moment at a time.

58.

Right livelihood is now a societal,
even planetary, responsibility.

—LEWIS RICHMOND

"Right livelihood" is part of the Buddhist Eightfold Path. The Buddha knew that work matters, personally and politically. The nature of our jobs and their impact on society and the environment is spiritual and ethical as well as economic. Good work brings joy to workers and sets them on a path toward enlightenment. Negative work—whether seen in terms of income, working condi-

tions, abuse and harassment, attitudes toward our jobs, or environmental destruction—stifles our spiritual lives and may put our souls at risk. Good work involves the commitment of a society to affirm working persons, compensate them fairly, and ensure that economics benefit worker, employer, and society alike.

Holy One, let me see my work and that of others as holy. As an opportunity to find meaning as well as spiritual growth. As a path toward social transformation and environmental healing. Remind me to give thanks to those whose work makes my well-being possible, justly protects my community, and provides comfort and security.

59.

Be perfect, therefore,
as your heavenly Parent is perfect.

—MATTHEW 5:48

Divine perfection, Jesus says, is found in God's intimate embrace of all creation, saint and sinner alike. Jesus' Sermon on the Mount describes an expansive God, who embraces friend and foe, provides sun and rain for the righteous and unrighteous, and has a stake in the ongoing processes of history and politics. With a bias toward justice, committed to the Earth and earthly existence, God's vision is for Shalom to be realized on "Earth as it is in Heaven."

There is nothing outside God's love. Nor should there be anything outside our loving concern. Our "perfection" consists in our ability to see holiness in all creation, most especially those we might view as foes, and then act accordingly. As we grow to be more like God in our ethical scope, our world expands, and our sense of responsibility embraces the whole Earth. While some may oppose us, and we may have to enter the hardscrabble world of protest and politics, we grow toward a "more perfect union" as we affirm solidarity and kinship with neighbor and stranger, friend and foe.

Spirit of All Creation, give me a heart as big as the universe. Give me the strength to experience others' pain. The courage to confront evil. And the insight to respond with wisdom, compassion, and pragmatic love to the evils I deplore.

60.

Give light and people will find the way.

—ELLA BAKER

There's an old saying that goes like this: "It is better to light a candle than to curse the darkness." Just one candle can provide light for the journey ahead, light that others can follow as well as ourselves. Gautama Buddha counseled: "Be light to yourselves." Jesus told his followers: "You are light of the world."

God's light can flow through us to bring light to the world. May our light shine so that pilgrims lost in the chaos can find their way!

Loving Spirit, help me be a light-bearer. Let my light shine, showing the path ahead for fellow travelers. Let my light bring life and love wherever I go as we travel together toward Your Promised Land of Shalom.

61.

For if you keep silence at such a time as this,
relief and deliverance will rise
for the Jews from another quarter,
but you and your father's family will perish.
Who knows?
Perhaps you have come to royal dignity
for just such a time as this.

—ESTHER 4:14

Mordecai calls Queen Esther to action for "just such a time as this." The queen has been lying low, keeping her Jewish identity secret in a time of persecution. Mordecai, her mentor,

tells her that now is the time to be an agent in the destiny of her people. Esther springs into action and taking her own initiative, planning her own course of action, saves her people.

Every time and place has a vocation—every moment has a vocation. We are alive, with all our gifts and limitations, for "just such a time as this." In an interdependent universe, we cannot sit on the sidelines. This is our time to be good ancestors and to make decisions that will shape for the good the lives of our descendants. This is the time! This is our time!

Loving Creator, awaken me to my vocation for just such a time as this. Let me plant seeds of healing for today and decades to come.

62.

At some moment I did answer
Yes to Someone—or something—
and from that hour I was certain
that existence is meaningful
and, that, therefore, my life,
in self-surrender, had a goal.
From that moment I have known what it means
"not to look back" and
"to take no thought for the morrow."

—DAG HAMMARSKJOLD

Do you remember saying "yes" to a particular vocational call? Life—or shall we call it God?—questions us every day. A door opens; will we walk through? An invitation comes; will we respond positively? A choice is required; will we choose the life-giving option? A threat is made; will we choose courage? When we say "yes," not fully knowing the outcome, we, like former United Nations General Secretary Dag Hammarskjold, will experience new direction and purpose, and the future will be filled with the spirit of "Yes."

When You call, Spirit of Possibility, give me the courage to say "yes" and move forward toward the far horizons You have prepared for me.

63.

The mystic commits him- or herself
to the removal of all
that prevents God from coming....
Whatever there is that blocks this,
calls for action.

—HOWARD THURMAN

God is constantly reaching out to us. The Divine call comes to real people in real time in real-life situations. We can open or turn away from God's call. We can also be prevented from hearing God's call by our family or political situation.

Howard Thurman lamented that one of the great tragedies of poverty and racism is the stifling of children's imaginations. Unjust systems threaten to undermine persons' experiences of the holy. Mystics—persons who encounter the Living God—experience God's inspiration to challenge any social policy that stifles abundant life. In prayerful protest and peaceful political change, we open the doors to creativity, imagination, and freedom for all God's children.

Loving Spirit, may my own experience of Your love inspire me to break down any impediment to abundant living among Your children.

64.

Then that little man in black there
[pointing to a priest],
he says women can't have
as much rights as men,
'cause Christ wasn't a woman!
Where did your Christ come from?
... From God and a woman!
Man had nothing to do with Him.

—SOJOURNER TRUTH

Abolitionist and women's rights activist Sojourner Truth proclaimed the radical message of God's incarnation in the Christ Child and in our lives. Born of a woman, Jesus blesses all women. The womb that bears Jesus bears all humankind. The wondrous diversity of sexuality—he, she, they—bears the Divine imprint.

The incarnation of Christ equalizes all humankind and makes everyone a manifestation of the Divine Spirit, even when we are unaware of it. Uplifting womankind uplifts humankind. All are one, yet many, in the Creator's wondrous fecundity.

Loving Spirit, may Christ be born in me. Show by Your love how I can be a midwife of Divinity in all its wondrous diversity.

65.

For all of you who were baptized
into union with Christ
clothed yourselves with Christ.
There is neither Judean nor Greek, slave nor
free, male and female;
for in Christ Jesus you are all one.

—GALATIANS 3:27–28

Unity and diversity are at the heart of reality. We are one in the Spirit, and yet each of us individually reflects Christ, and we are also many

in God's creativity. This wondrous polarity is built into creation. Unique, we are joined. Joined in Christ, we reflect the giftedness of "trinitarian" diversity. Recognizing the pluralistic unity of life inspires us to honor and support the wondrous giftedness of each cell in the "Body of Christ" and the importance of each cell's well-being in the Body's health. Let us see only Christ, only the holiness of the other, as we also affirm the wondrous and diverse garments with which they are clothed.

Wise and Dynamic Creator, Source of Unity, and Parent of Plurality, help me to hold in loving contrast the one and the many embodied at every level of life.

66.

A person is ethical when life
as such is sacred to him—
the life of plants and animals—
as well as his fellow men
and when he devotes himself to all life
that is in need of help.

—ALBERT SCHWEITZER

Albert Schweitzer asserted that "reverence for life" is the most fundamental ethical principle. Every living organism calls us to be amazed and appreciative. We are standing on holy ground wherever we step. The starry night, the newborn

child, the grandchild sleeping beside you, your life companion of many decades, a breaching whale, a plodding pangolin, a racing Golden Doodle—all reveal Divine artistry and love.

Yes, there is competition among species and human communities for supremacy. Still, Divine creativity bursts forth, though often disguised in conflict. The beauty and pain of life call us to reverence, and reverence challenges us to value life itself and commit ourselves to bringing joy to our human and nonhuman companions.

Fill me with radical amazement at each creature's existence, Spirit. Let my amazement lead to love and protection and stewardship of our small blue-green planet.

67.

> Today it is not merely enough to be a saint,
> but we must have the saintliness
> demanded by the present moment,
> a new saintliness without precedent.
>
> —SIMONE WEIL

Mystic and activist Simone Weil challenges us to be saints in our time of social media, immediate global communication, global climate change, growing social incivility, and racial injustice. Saints, like mystics, wish to shape their lives around experiencing God in daily life, in the

faces of foe and friend alike, in the nonhuman world as well as the human—and then respond to every life form with a sense of reverence and affirmation. Like Johnny Appleseed, saints plant seeds of Divinity wherever they walk, delighting in God's call in their lives and seeking to be God's intimate companions in healing the Earth.

Loving Spirit, I thank You for each creature's unique experience and value, knowing I am always on holy ground. Let me spread holiness wherever I go to bring healing to all creation.

68.

Our Parent in heaven, hallowed be your name.
Your kingdom come. Your will be done,
on earth as it is in heaven.
Give us this day our daily bread.

—MATTHEW 6:9-11

The Lord's Prayer joins Heaven and Earth. Heavenly values—God's vision of Shalom, peace, and justice—are to become earthly realities, and the quest for peace and justice must begin with those who call themselves God's followers. God's followers are to heavenly minded and

earthly good. We are to be guided by God's vision and then enact that vision on Earth, beginning with daily bread for others as well as ourselves.

Our planet is chockful of Divinity. God's grandeur, as Gerard Manley Hopkins wrote, is revealed in the "dearest freshness deep down things" and in the "pied beauty" of creation's wondrous multiplicity. Let us awaken to Divine beauty, and in recognizing life and its Creator, we will give God the glory by sharing the bread of life with our human companions and treasuring the nonhuman world.

Spirit, whose love joins Heaven and Earth, may my loyalty to You radiate to all creation.

69.

It all boils down to this,
that all life is interrelated.
We are caught in an inescapable
network of mutuality,
tied into a single garment of destiny....
We are made to live together
because of the interrelated structure of reality.

—MARTIN LUTHER KING JR.

Ubuntu: I am because of you. As Francis Thompson avers, "Thou canst not stir a flower without troubling a star." We are, despite Cain's protests, our siblings' keepers. Their lives depend

on us, and without our siblings and the support of the planet, we could not exist for a moment.

The self-made person is a fantasy. We create one another. Our achievements affirm one another. Our misdeeds add to the suffering of the planet. In the graceful interdependence of life, let us cherish our own unique beauty, make our lives a gift to God and others, and give thanks to our Creator and to those whose lives have made the amazing uniqueness of this moment possible.

Thank You! Thank You! Thank you! Out of thanksgiving, let me spread love and bring justice to the Earth and its creatures, for we are one.

70.

> For some strange reason
> I cannot be what I ought to be
> until you are what you ought to be.
> And you can never be what you ought to be
> until I am what I ought to me.
> That's the way God's universe is made.
>
> —MARTIN LUTHER KING JR.

Deep down, we all depend on each other. Deep down, we can all nurture each other. Moral and spiritual maturity involves moving from self-interest—the isolated ego and its well-being—to global concern and loyalty to the planet and its peoples.

Sacrificing for the greater good is at the heart of morality. The planet calls us to expand our circle of love from family, to close friendships, community, nation, and the planet. We are all in this together. Our quality of life is grounded in mutuality, despite the attempts of the "self-made" to deny this. The graceful interdependence of life is the foundation for loving relationships that embrace the whole Earth.

Loving Spirit, I cannot exist for a moment without Your care and support—and I cannot exist without the support of others and the environment. Help me to see my connections, and bring love and beauty to each encounter.

71.

Don't ask what the world needs.
Ask what makes you come alive, and go do it.
Because what the world needs
is people who have come alive.

—HOWARD THURMAN

What makes you come alive? What are you passionate about? To paraphrase Frederick Buechner, your vocation is the place where your passions meet the world's needs. You also experience God's passions when you are in the zone of doing what you are called to do. Each moment is filled with possibility and the energy to embody your dreams and passions in real life.

Each life has holy energies waiting to burst forth. In our intricately connected universe, our passions are meant for others as well as ourselves. Our joys and delights merge with the experiences of others, creating a healing field of force that radiates far beyond ourselves. Let us have a lively passionate commitment to embody God's passions in our daily lives and social commitment.

**Awaken me, Spirit, to passion and love.
Let my passions flow in healing acts for all humankind and all creation.**

72.

Thank God that in other countries peasants
are plowing and planting
and doing new things—
all of them samples of heaven,
all of them portents
of that new heaven and new earth
where justice dwelleth.

—DOROTHY DAY

Gratitude can be an inspiration to justice-seeking. During the pandemic, I often remembered the "essential workers," many of whom were unheralded, others undocumented immigrants. Paid low wages and subject to deportation from

an ungrateful nation, their hands and feet made it possible for me to have food on my table. Gratitude is appropriate for health-care workers and first responders and also for warehouse workers, store clerks, truck drivers, and farmworkers.

Gratitude inspires us to seek fair wages, working conditions, and bargaining rights for all workers, and citizenship for the undocumented immigrants who provide our food. Thanksgiving becomes real when we work for just social structures and respect for all those who ensure our well-being.

Thank You, Spirit, for the "essential workers" who toil daily that I might enjoy safety, health, and nutrition. Make my gratitude real as I seek justice and respect for all who labor.

73.

> We want them to feel that they are wanted. . . .
> We want them to know that there are people
> who really love them, who really want them . . .
> to know human and divine love.
>
> —MOTHER TERESA

There is a saying circulated among ministers and other caring professionals: "They don't care what you know until they know that you care." Those in need of societal justice don't need our pity. They don't need to be pointed out as objects of our charity or paternalistic public

policies. They need our love. They need our sense of solidarity, not superiority. They need to be the apple of our eyes, our siblings, our fellow mortals.

A plaque at a Paris hospital has struck me as especially insightful: "We are the dying caring for the dying." We are also the vulnerable caring for the vulnerable. We are the needy caring for the needy. Our privilege and prosperity are fleeting, just as our lives are.

Link me with all humanity, Spirit, so that my generosity is grounded in unity and my charity rooted in companionship.

74.

Do not let the behavior of others
destroy your inner peace.

—DALAI LAMA

Psychiatrist and Holocaust survivor Viktor Frankl asserted that "everything can be taken from a [person] but one thing: the last of the human freedoms—to choose one's attitude in any given set of circumstances, to choose one's own way." From a place of inner calm emerges creative responses to systemic violence and social injustice.

The path to peace is fraught with setbacks and conflict. We may be the object of insult and

threat. Failure may dog our steps. Peace comes, though, through being a center in the cyclone, a still point in the turning world. A commitment to inner peace becomes a crucible enabling us to face failure as well as success without hate, polarization, incivility, and fear. Peace emerges when we trust our inner resources, grounded in an affirmation of the goodness of life and the sustaining resources of the Divine. As the hymn witnesses: "No storm can shake my inmost calm / While to that rock I'm clinging / Since love is Lord of heaven and earth / How can I keep from singing?"

Let Your peace give me calm in the storm. Let me remember that there is no way to peace, for peace is the way.

75.

Nobody's free until everybody's free.

—FANNY LOU HAMER

Civil rights activist Fanny Lou Hamer affirmed the solidarity of life. Persons of privilege often make no connection between their prosperity and the poverty of others. In their privilege and prosperity, they also forget that their spiritual well-being is dependent on the liberation of others.

Freedom and justice are indivisible. Lives broken by systemic injustice destroy the soul of the nation. Structural injustice not only ruins physical lives but also puts at risk the spiritual

lives of the privileged and powerful and those who oppress the poor. There is a freedom that emerges when we open our doors to the horizons of hope for those who have been outsiders. There is a lightness of spirit that arises when the gains of others contribute to our success. Set free from our spiritual prisons, we become companions on a journey to freedom.

Let the spirit of freedom flow in and through me, joining me with justice-seekers and peacemakers everywhere in the quest for a world where freedom rings in every neighborhood and urban setting, farm and village.

76.

If a child grows up with the idea of violence,
that you get what you can by force,
what kind of world will this be?

—JULINDA ABU NASR

Lebanese educator, feminist, and children's advocate, Julinda Abu Nasr recognizes the importance of parenting for peace and justice. Violence births violence. Hate breeds hate. Incivility begets alienation. Parents, grandparents, and congregations must be teachers of peace. We must learn to resolve conflict while staying in relationship. We must learn to speak the truth

with great love. Teaching peace is grounded in "being peace," that is, being examples of peace-making, rooted in our commitment to truth and reconciliation. Peace teaching comes from bathing our children and grandchildren in love, respect, and affirmation, while modeling loving relationships. Peace, a sense of Shalom, takes us from self-interest to world loyalty and inspires us to pass these virtues to our children.

When children see me, Spirit, may they see peace, compassion, generosity, and love that build bridges toward all.

77.

The Bible has been used as a way
of making us accept our situation,
and not to bring enlightenment to the poor.

—RIGOBERTA MENCHU

The Bible is a revolutionary text and yet it has been used to maintain the status quo. Slaves have been told to obey their masters. Women have been required to be subservient to their husbands. Impoverished people have been told to defer the quest for justice to the afterlife. LGBTQ communities have been ostracized and told to stay in the shadows. Indigenous cultures

have been decimated, with the scriptures used as tools of subjugation. In contrast, authentic biblical spirituality is prophetic, challenging us to transform the social order.

Biblical spirituality inspires us to pray and protest, to sacrifice our privilege for the greater good. Let us be guided by the prophetic spirit of Jesus: "to bring good news to the poor ... release to the captives ... recovery of sight to the blind ... freedom to the oppressed ... and proclaim God's realm of Shalom" (Luke 4:18–19).

Spirit, let my faith inspire creative restlessness and discontent with the status quo. May my faith agitate my comfort and inspire me to champion the cause of the oppressed.

78.

You can pray until you faint,
but unless you get up and try to do something,
God is not going to put it in your lap.

—FANNY LOU HAMER

Prayer awakens us to the joy and pain of our neighbors and invites us to get up from our easy chairs to do that one—in our eyes, often small—act that will change someone's life and create the circumstances for the achievement of justice in our community. Prayer is an act of the imagination, taking us beyond self-interest to love our neighbor, and beyond passivity to unite

with the power that creates the universe. Effective prayer lures us forward into action toward the far horizons of Shalom.

Loving Spirit, show me how I can be an agent of justice. Awaken my heart to pain— and then energize me to do something today that will tip the balance toward the world You imagine for me and this good Earth.

79.

I believe that peace is not merely
an absence of war,
but the nurture of human life,
and that in time this nurture
will do away with war as a natural process.

—JANE ADDAMS

Social activist, champion of women's equality, and one of the founders of the American Civil Liberties Union, Jane Addams recognized that the quest for peace requires a commitment to justice and equality at every level of life. Peace is the presence of wholeness, not the absence of conflict.

The quest for peace and the challenge of injustice may create conflicts. These conflicts, however, are temporary processes aimed at the health of the organism—the community. Distinctions will continue to exist in terms of religion, race, talent, gifts, and interests, and these differences will be affirmed in the dynamic realization of the Peaceable Realm.

Let me rejoice, Spirit, in the symphony of diverse cultures, the mosaic of hues, the chorale of different gifts and talents.

80.

> We become not a melting pot
> but a beautiful mosaic.
> Different people, different beliefs,
> different yearnings,
> different hopes, different dreams.
>
> —PRESIDENT JIMMY CARTER

Divinity gives birth to diversity. The Holy Trinity itself testifies to diversity as essential to God's character and everything God creates. Difference need not lead to division but can be the source of artistic and creative contrast. Our families and communities—our nations—grow

by affirming diversity as the source of innovation, growth, and creativity. The quest for creative diversity requires acceptance, affirmation, and acknowledgment—and the recognition that none of our perspectives and cultures is complete without the gifts of others. Let us rejoice in the glorious mosaic of our communities and nations.

Spirit, bless my world in all its wondrous diversity. Bless the many communities, cultures, races, and perspectives of my nation.

81.

Because we fail to listen to each other's stories,
we are becoming a fragmented human race.

—MADELEINE L'ENGLE

Jewish wisdom says God created humanity because God loves stories. Each of us has a story, but often our stories are hidden, deemed unimportant, or silenced. It has been said that history is written by the victorious. Today, however, we need history, herstory, and their story, emerging from symphonies of voices. In hearing another's story of joy and sorrow, success and

failure, our minds open to larger realities and our hearts beat in empathy. In welcoming stories of groups whose voices have been silenced or forgotten, we gain a sense of unity that leads to affirmation and solidarity.

Pause, ask, listen, and truly hear the voice of holiness in a child's tales, a grandparent's recollections, an immigrant's pilgrimage, or a stranger's adventures. In hearing stories of joy, woe, pain, and aspiration, we find common cause, discover our essential unity, and move from apathy to empathy and action.

Give me a listening heart, O Spirit. Let me open my mind and heart to Your voice in others' voices and Your hopes in their hopes.

82.

If you are free, you need to free somebody else.
If you have some power,
then your job is to empower somebody else.

—TONI MORRISON

Noted author Toni Morrison spoke these words to her students. With the grand tradition of Western education beginning with Pythagoras and Plato, she saw education as a lifelong process of spiritual growth.

Education grows roots and wings: it roots us in our current world and sends us toward the future with wings of possibility. The freedoms

and achievements of our education do not solely belong to us, nor are they the result of our efforts alone. They emerge from an intricate interpersonal, institutional, and inspirational ecology in which our challenge is to give as we have received. Having received the gift of freedom and power, we work to share that freedom and power with others. We don't live in a zero-sum world in which your gain is my loss. We live in a creative exponential world in which when one of us makes authentic gains, we all grow and prosper.

Holy One, inspire me to use my gifts to bring abundance to others.

83.

When my mother had prayed with me
and kissed me goodnight,
I used to add silently a prayer
that I had composed myself
for all living creatures. It ran thus:
"O heavenly Father protect and bless
all things that have breath;
guard them from all evil,
and let them sleep in peace."

—ALBERT SCHWEITZER

Too often our spirituality has focused only on human concerns. We have created binary divisions between environmentalists and social activists and contemplatives and protesters. Today, we speak of contemplative activism and ecojustice, recognizing that peace and justice relate to all creation, not just humankind. Our well-being is connected to the health of ecosystems and species. As young Albert Schweitzer realized, existence itself is holy and deserves our ethical consideration. Let our prayers expand in circles of compassion, encompassing all humanity in its diversity, and extending to embrace the whole Earth.

God of All Creation, bless all creatures, domestic as well as wild.

84.

We need the stars. . . . We need purpose!
We need the image of Destiny
to take root among the stars
gives us of ourselves as a purposeful,
growing species.
We need to become the adult species
that the Destiny can help us become!

—OCTAVIA BUTLER

Science fiction author Octavia Butler reminds us that we need to dream big. We need the stars. We need the far horizon. We need challenges that require all the energy and hope we can muster.

Aiming small leads to mediocrity and perpetuates injustice. We need far horizons, impossible dreams, intergalactic journeys of heart and mind to propel us to seek realms of justice our parents could not imagine. Beyond the crises of the present moment are blue horizons of hope. Without that hope, we are mired in injustice. With hope, we soar to the stars and embody unimagined possibilities of healing and wholeness for our nation and planet.

Let us soar to the stars, Spirit, and aim toward the far horizon.

85.

Children have never been very good
at listening to their elders,
but they have never failed to imitate them.

—JAMES BALDWIN

Author and activist James Baldwin gives parents and grandparents their marching orders: he challenges us to walk the talk. We can talk about justice, but our talk is empty if we do not actively seek justice and peace. We can speak about the evils of racism, but our words are moot if we do not work to become anti-racists, confronting systemic injustice and examining white privilege.

Our children and grandchildren are watching! Let them see peace, hospitality, justice, and fairness in our interactions with others and citizens. Let us be wise elders and good ancestors, planting seeds of justice for their future.

Help me, Spirit, to walk the talk, being Your hands and feet and heart for peace and justice.

86.

We have to be braver than we think we can be,
because God is constantly calling us
to be more than we are.

—MADELEINE L'ENGLE

God is graceful and accepting; God loves us as we are—but God doesn't leave us where we are. Virtually every biblical encounter with God, from Moses to Isaiah and Mary of Magdala to Paul on the road to the Damascus, challenged people to go beyond their comfort zones. God doesn't want us to play small, to flatten our hopes and dreams. God wants us to reach for the

stars, to launch out in deep waters, to face our fears and limitations, to confront the glass ceiling and then break through it. In the quest for justice and peace in the twenty-first century, we must press beyond our limitations of imagination and agency.

The threats and conflicts threaten to overwhelm us. But our small group can be catalytic in our community. Our candle of hope can light the darkness.

Let me place my resources in Your hands, Spirit. Multiply them exponentially by Your grace to expand my heart and change the world.

87.

Make peace with the universe.
Take joy in it. Every moment, a new beauty.

—RUMI

The inner and outer life are intimately connected. In our vocation as peacemakers, our first responsibility involves deepening our spiritual lives. Coming to terms with the universe inspires both agency and acceptance. Accepting the wonders of the universe as well as its tragic beauty enables us to delight in the gifts of each new day. With the Serenity Prayer, we can accept the things we cannot change. We can also, as

activist Angela Davis urges, commit ourselves to using our agency to respond to what is in our power, "changing the things I cannot accept." Joy, calm, restlessness, acceptance, and challenge are not mutually exclusive. They reflect the deep peace that inspires compassion and prophetic healing.

Deep Peace of the Restless Sea, join calm with agitation, comfort with challenge, and care with confrontation. Help me to joyfully play my role in redeeming the world.

88.

Be a good ancestor.
Stand for something bigger than yourself.
Add value to the earth during your sojourn.

—MARIAN WRIGHT EDELMAN

As a grandparent, I know that life is not about me. My life is important, and I look forward to many good years of writing, teaching, traveling, and hiking—but I also recognize that future generations depend on me to be active in advocating for Earth care. Children of color need me to be a committed anti-racist so they can experience

liberty and justice. LGBTQ children depend on me to speak for justice and equality, and advocate for the protection of their rights.

Good ancestors know that their lives radiate across history. They live fully today, rejoicing in life and sharing their gifts with generations that they will never meet but whose quality of life depends on their good stewardship.

God of All Times and Places, help me to look beyond myself and act for the well-being of future generations.

89.

Be lights unto yourself.

— GAUTAMA BUDDHA

In his final speech, with death looming on the horizon, Gautama Buddha counseled his disciples to bring forth the light within. Discovering their individual lights, they could chart their own path and provide guidance to fellow pilgrims.

Justice-seeking and peacemaking must include our own inner work as well as our outer transformational activity. Discovering inner resources and resilience, we can tread the stony road toward jus-

tice with joy. Developing our inner light through contemplation, self-awareness, and challenge, we will be able to face failure and success in the quest for justice and peace with equanimity, claiming each person, whether "friend" or "foe," as a sibling.

Let me seek the light, Spirit, see the light, and share the light. Let my inner light flame forth to provide pathways to justice and peace for fellow pilgrims.

90.

Jesus says: "I am the light which is on them all.
I am the All, and the All has gone out from me
and the All has come back to me.
Cleave the wood: I am there;
lift the stone and thou shalt find me there!"

—THE GOSPEL OF THOMAS

Like Buddha, Jesus treasured the inner light. He recognized that when we realize we are the light of the world, we can let our light shine in service to others. He knew that the bright light of spiritual liberation reaches beyond individual

enlightenment. God's light is not solely our possession but is the deepest reality of all creation, the bedrock of human existence. As light-bearers, our task is to reveal the light within others. We can take courage in the wisdom of the spiritual: "This little light of mine, I'm gonna let it shine."

Awaken my senses, Spirit, to the flame in all things—and let my light shine, shine!

91.

I should like a great lake
of finest ale for the King of kings.
I should like a table of the choicest food
for the family of heaven. . . .
I should welcome the poor to my feast,
for they are God's children.
I should welcome the sick to my feast,
for they are God's joy.

—ST. BRIGID

Justice is about Jubilee! Peacemaking is about celebration! The goal of justice-seeking and peacemaking is to uplift the planet, creating a feast open to all God's children, providing everything we need to prosper. No one is left behind at the Divine smorgasbord. God is the giver and we are the messengers and providers. As Mahatma Gandhi said, "The world has enough for everyone's need, not everyone's greed."

In giving, we receive. In blessing, we are blessed. In sharing, we experience abundance.

Spirit of Celebration and Compassion, let us rejoice and celebrate, sharing with one another the bounties of Your good Earth.

92.

Become the change you want to see in the world.

— MAHATMA GANDHI

We don't have to wait for others to change to make significant changes in our own lives. We don't have to wait for politicians or even religious leaders to show us the way. God is already at work in our lives giving us the wisdom and energy to respond to the crises at hand. As Rabbi Hillel, who lived in the century before Jesus, wrote: "If I am not for myself—who will be? If I am only for myself—what am I? If not now—when?"

Remember the power of one person acting with courage and integrity: Ruby Bridges walks to school breaking color barriers in the United States, Rosa Parks refuses to move to another seat, Greta Thunberg initiates Friday strikes to confront global climate change, the Parkland High School kids go on the road to protest against gun violence. You too have the opportunity to do something transformative for God. You can take the first steps, appropriate to your life situation, to reconcile with opposing groups. You can be the change you want to see in the world.

Give me wisdom and courage, Spirit, to know what I am called to do—and then take the first steps to do it.

93.

The aim of the universe
is toward the production of beauty.

—ALFRED NORTH WHITEHEAD

There is an arc toward beauty in the universe. Looking out from the Hubble Space Telescope, we are awestruck at the lively and intricate world of galaxies and black holes. Looking at our own planet, we can delight at multicolored flora and the millions of species emerging on our planet. Evolution is not just the survival of the fittest; it also involves the aim toward complexity, creativity, and cooperation.

When Mother Teresa said, "Do something beautiful for God," she recognized that our acts of kindness and beauty can add to God's evolving beauty. Our work for peace and justice makes possible greater creativity, artistry, self-determination, possibility, and joy for others. When we support vulnerable persons and ensure a healthy planet for future generations, we can rejoice because, as God's hands and feet, we are letting the beauty of the universe flow in and through us, partnering with God in this glorious and beautiful world.

Let me be a love-finder and beauty-creator, Spirit, adding the music of my own heart to the symphony of life.

94.

> Nothing that is worth doing
> can be achieved in our lifetime;
> therefore we must be saved by hope. . . .
> Nothing we do, however virtuous,
> can be accomplished alone;
> therefore we must be saved by love.
>
> —REINHOLD NIEBUHR

American theologian Reinhold Niebuhr reminds us that our calling is to be faithful to our ideals, to do the work that is needed, to love greatly,

and challenge injustice courageously—and then leave the future in the hands of God. We can't ensure success. Living with our limitations in power, wisdom, and achievement, we go forward, uncertain of the outcome, recognizing that our efforts are supplemented by others and that in seeking goodness and beauty, we are embodying God's vision in our place and time.

Recognizing my limits, let me do the job in front of me, Spirit. Let me fulfill the vocation of this moment in time, leaving what I cannot finish to others and trusting Your eternal love.

95.

Search me, O God, and know my heart;
test me and know my thoughts.
See if there is any wicked way in me,
and lead me in the way everlasting.

—PSALM 139:23-24

Self-awareness, or mindfulness, is at the heart of justice-seeking and peacemaking. Our knowledge of ourselves nurtures our gifts and promotes resilience. It also helps us respond to our ethical, spiritual, and experiential limitations. Knowing our own tendencies toward hatred, violence, and incivility enables us to rise

above these tendencies, transforming them into humble and righteous protest and hardscrabble prophetic healing. Self-awareness in the political arena makes it possible for us to advocate for peace and justice without coming to resemble those whom we oppose in tactics and behavior. Self-awareness opens the door to embodying both prophetic protest and relational healing.

Search my heart, Spirit, examine my motives, and heal my hatred and intolerance.

96.

We are the ones we have been waiting for.

—JUNE JORDAN

Poet June Jordan commemorated 40,000 South African women and children who, on August 9, 1956, put their bodies on the line to protest the inhumanity of state-sanctioned apartheid, reminding us that we can't wait for others to change the world. We need to be change agents in the here and now. Each person has a calling for "just such a time as this" to be faithful in the quest for justice for themselves and for others.

Our vocation is to respond to the evils of our time, rather than pronounce platitudes and do

nothing. I must admit that this is challenging for me. I am more of a contemplative than a prophet. And yet, I am called to speak out for justice and peace in my time and place even if it means leaving my comfort zone and risking conflict. Racial justice can't wait. Care for the vulnerable and poor can't wait. Earth care can't wait. The time is now, and God calls us to speak and act, for "we are the ones we have been waiting for."

Loving Spirit, energize my hands and feet, voice and heart, mind and skills.

97.

The steadfast love of the Lord never ceases,
his mercies never come to an end;
they are new every morning;
great is your faithfulness.
"The Lord is my portion," says my soul,
"therefore I will hope in him."

—LAMENTATIONS 3:22-24

The world is constantly changing—and in all the changes, God is faithful. God never stands still, for Divine faithfulness is revealed in mercies that are new every morning.

In life's challenges, let us be hopeful, knowing that God's vision charts the course of history. God propels the moral and spiritual arcs whose presence energizes and transforms our lives and the world.

Loving Spirit, Your mercies are eternal and yet new every morning. Your love is constantly responding to my deepest needs and my quest for justice. Give me hope and courage for the living of these days.

98.

My job now is prayer.

—DOROTHY DAY

To some, prayer reflects passivity and makes little or no difference in terms of social transformation. Social activist Dorothy Day took a different approach. Sidelined by declining health and no longer able to protest, lecture, or be arrested for nonviolent civil disobedience, she realized that prayer was now her vocation.

Prayer changes us and changes the world. It orients our hearts toward God's vision. Even when

we can no longer be activists—or during a time of pandemic, when our activism is curtailed—our prayers radiate across the planet, changing the spiritual temperature of our planet. Our prayers sustain other, more public activists, providing them with extra energy, patience, and insight.

When we cannot picket, let us pray. When protest is impossible for us, let our prayers bring life and light to the world.

Loving Spirit, give me the patience of prayer. Let my prayers sustain my spirit and uplift justice-seekers everywhere. Let my prayers energize and nurture the poor and vulnerable.

99.

Deep peace of the running wave to you
Deep peace of the flowing air to you
Deep peace of the quiet earth to you
Deep peace of the shining stars to you
Deep peace of the gentle night to you. . . .
Deep peace of Christ to you.

—CELTIC BLESSING

There is a deep peace in our restless, evolving universe. Amid life's transitions and uncertainties, the bedrock of Divine peace undergirds our personal and political quests for peace. We are part of a universe story, stretching back 14

billion years and containing a trillion galaxies. Our planet and our lives flicker briefly in light of eternity. Yet what we do matters. We are part of God's story and the deep reality of peace that sustains all creation. Our efforts are finite, but our failures are never final. What we do is never lost and shares in God's everlasting life. Aware of our limits, let us take our place as God's companions in healing the Earth.

Brief though my life is and finite though my achievements may be, let me do my part, Spirit, and fulfill my vocation as Your companion in healing the Earth.

100.

My religion is very simple.
My religion is kindness.

—DALAI LAMA

These days religion is used to divide communities and conquer opponents. The crusade mentality of saved versus unsaved, friend versus foe, and loyal versus disloyal populates our pulpits and impacts American politics. There is another way, though: the pathway of healing and kindness, grounded in perceiving all creation as kin.

Difference is real and must be recognized, especially by persons of privilege. Still, a kind

religion aims at unity, healing, and wholeness. A kind religion goes beyond the binary to recognize that there is no "other."

Let us pledge ourselves to kindness as well as truth and justice. May we compromise when necessary and let go of self-interest to promote healing.

Loving Spirit, whose love accepts me in my imperfections, keep me on the path to kindness.

101.

We are called to be a movement
for wholeness in a broken world.

—MISSION STATEMENT,
CHRISTIAN CHURCH
(DISCIPLES OF CHRIST)

We know the brokenness of the world. It sometimes appears intractable. The problems are larger than our resources. When we band together as a community, however, our singular cells become a body, and our drops of experience become an ever-flowing stream.

Look deeply at the world around you. Peer into the eyes and listen to the words of people you encounter. There are persons waiting for your companionship as world-healers. There are persons whom you can bless with your life and from whom you will receive a glorious blessing. Like yourself, they may feel alone and powerless. Together we become a movement that brings healing and wholeness to our broken world.

Spirit of Healing Love, show me the people and groups that I can join in solidarity to change the world. Help me encounter companions who will inspire me to service and who will see my life as an inspiration to their quest for wholeness.

About the Author

The grandparent of two elementary school boys, with whom he learns and plays daily, Bruce Epperly is a Cape Cod pastor, professor, and author of over 50 books, including *Become Fire: Guideposts for Postmodern Pilgrims, Spirit Online: A Mystic's Guide to the Internet, Thin Places Everywhere: The 12 Days of Christmas with Celtic Christianity,* and *101 Soul Seeds for Grandparents Working for a Better World.*

101 Soul Seeds

for Parents of Adult Children

Being a parent held joys and challenges every step of the way, and never more so than when our children finally made it to adulthood. Now we can connect with them on deeper levels than ever—but unexpected potential pitfalls dot this new path we're traveling. *101 Soul Seeds for Parents of Adult Children* offers observations and quotes, coupled with simple prayers to help us navigate this portion of parenting . . . so we and our adult children grow closer to one another and closer to our own souls' destination.

Paperback Price: $12.99

Kindle Price: $4.99

101 Soul Seeds

for Grandparents Working for a Better World

Grandparenting is truly a holy adventure. As we see and bring forth the inner divinity of our grandchildren, we have the opportunity to show them that they are not only our beloved grandchildren but God's children as well, infinite in worth and possibility.

This book is an invitation to consider grandparenting as a spiritual and ethical vocation. As we commit ourselves to love and pray for our grandchildren, we can also work to create a just and healthy world for all grandchildren.

Paperback Price: $12.99

Kindle Price: $4.99

Anamchara Books

www.AnamcharaBooks.com

www.ingramcontent.com/pod-product-compliance
Lightning Source LLC
Chambersburg PA
CBHW060521080526
44586CB00012B/570